The "HOW DID WE FIND OUT . . . ?" series
by Isaac Asimov

HOW DID WE FIND OUT—

How Did We
Find Out About
Photosynthesis?

How Did We
Find Out About
Photosynthesis?

Isaac Asimov

Illustrated by Erika Kors

Walker and Company
New York

First published in the United States of America in 1989
by the Walker Publishing Company, Inc.

Published simultaneously in Canada by Thomas Allen & Son
Canada, Limited, Markham, Ontario.

Library of Congress Cataloging-in-Publication Data

Asimov, Isaac, 1920–
    How did we find out about photosynthesis? / Isaac Asimov ;
illustrated by Erika Kors.
        p.   cm.—(How did we find out—series)
    Includes index.
    Summary: Traces the scientific discoveries that led to our
understanding of photosynthesis and how this process relates to the
food supply, changing ecological balance, and threats to the Earth's
atmosphere.
    ISBN 0-8027-6899-7 (trade)   0-8027-6886-5 (lib. bdg.)
    1. Photosynthesis—Research—History—Juvenile literature.
2. Photosynthesis—Juvenile literature   [1. Photosynthesis.]
I. Kors, Erika W., ill.   II. Title.   III. Series: Asimov, Isaac,
1920–   How did we find out—series.
QK882.A79   1989
581.1'3342—dc20   89-5832
                                                              CIP
                                                              AC

Printed in the United States of America

10 9 8 7 6 5 4 3 2 1

Dedicated to
the memory of Heinz Pagels (1939–1988)

Contents

1
Oxygen

WE ALL BREATHE. We draw air into our lungs and then puff it out again.

The air we breath is one-fifth *oxygen* (OK-sih-jen), and it is these atoms of oxygen that we use. We combine oxygen with substances in the body that contain *carbon* (KAHR-bon) and *hydrogen* (HY-druh-jen). The carbon combines with oxygen to form carbon dioxide (KAHR-bon-dy-OK-side). The hydrogen combines with oxygen to form water.

When we breathe out, then, the air from our lungs is missing some of the oxygen it had when we breathed in. Instead, we breathe out carbon dioxide and water vapor. This process is called *respiration*

(RES-pih-RAY-shun), from Latin words meaning "to breathe over and over."

We're breathing all the time. So are all people and all other animals. People and other animals have been breathing for many millions of years. Why hasn't all the oxygen in the air been used up by now? Why hasn't it all been replaced by carbon dioxide and water?

And how about the substances in the body that provide carbon and hydrogen? If we keep combining them with the oxygen we breathe, why don't we use them up?

To replace the carbon and hydrogen, we eat food that contains those atoms. But where does the carbon and hydrogen in the food come from? We eat different kinds of plants, such as fruits and vegetables. We also eat animals, such as cattle, hogs, and chickens that, in turn, eat plants. The carbon and hydrogen, in the end, come from plants, which end up as food for all the animals of the world, one way or another.

But where do the plants get the carbon and hydrogen? They don't eat.

Those are the two big questions: How do we breathe without using up all the air? How do we eat without using up all the food?

Plants are easier to study than air is. At least you can see plants and watch them grow. They won't grow unless you plant them in soil and water them. It seems, therefore, that either soil or water (or both) has to turn into plant material as plants grow.

In 1643, a Belgian scientist, Jan Baptista van Helmont (HEL-mont, 1577–1644), thought he would decide the matter by experiment. He weighed out a quantity of soil and planted a willow tree in it. He kept the pot of soil covered so that nothing could get into it except the water he put in himself. He watered that tree for five years and then carefully uprooted it and knocked all the soil off the roots back into the pot.

Helmont found that the willow tree weighed 164 pounds, but the soil had lost only two ounces. He decided that it was not the soil that turned into plant material. It was the water.

In Helmont's time, however, it was not known that different kinds of atoms exist in different materials. Helmont didn't know that water contains only hydrogen and oxygen atoms, while plants contains hydrogen, oxygen, and carbon atoms.

But then, soil and water were not the only things that touched the willow tree Helmont had grown. Air had touched it, too, but Helmont didn't take that into account. Hardly anyone did in those days. You can't see or feel air, so people usually ignored it.

Yet Helmont did study air, though not in connection with his willow tree. He was the first to notice that there are different kinds of air. Because the different airs are invisible and don't have any shape, Helmont thought they resembled something the ancient Greeks called *chaos* (KAY-os), meaning all jumbled up and shapeless. Helmont pronounced the word in his own language and it became *gas*. To this day, we speak of air and other airlike substances as gases.

Helmont found that when he burned wood, a gas quite different from ordinary air was produced. Things wouldn't burn in this gas from wood as they

Jan Baptista van Helmont

would burn in air. The new gas dissolved in water, which ordinary air would not. The gas Helmont studied is the one we now call carbon dioxide.

It turns out that carbon dioxide is very important to plant growth, but Helmont never realized that.

Other scientists grew interested in gases. A British scientist, Stephen Hales (1677–1761), studied them in detail, and, in 1727, he wondered if a gas might be involved in plant growth. However, he couldn't figure out which particular gas might be the one.

Then, in 1756, another British scientist, Joseph Black (1728–1799), studied carbon dioxide and found that it combined with a mineral called *lime*, changing it into another called *limestone*.

Then he noticed that he did not have to expose the lime to carbon dioxide. If he just let the lime stand in ordinary air, it very slowly began to undergo the change. This meant there was carbon dioxide in the air around us; maybe just a little bit, but it was there.

In 1772, still another British scientist, Daniel Rutherford (RUTH-er-ford, 1749–1819), burned a candle in a closed container of air. After a while, the candle went out and burned no more. It was known by then that a burning candle produces carbon dioxide. That made it seem as though the candle had used all the air and had replaced it with carbon dioxide.

However, carbon dioxide combines with certain chemicals. By adding those chemicals to the gas in the container Rutherford got rid of all the carbon dioxide. That still left plenty of gas in the container, but a candle would not burn in that remaining gas.

Rutherford decided that air contained a gas that was

not carbon dioxide and that things would not burn in it. Eventually, that gas was named *nitrogen* (NITE-ruh-jen).

Then, in 1774, yet another British scientist, Joseph Priestley (PREEST-lee, 1733–1804), obtained from air a gas in which objects burned furiously. If placed into this gas, a thin piece of wood that was merely smoldering would instantly burst into flame. The gas was eventually named oxygen.

Finally, in 1775, a French scientist, Antoine Laurent Lavoisier (la-vwah-ZYAY, 1743–1794), put all this together. He said that air is a mixture of two gases. It is about $4/5$ nitrogen and $1/5$ oxygen. It is the oxygen that makes things burn in air and it is the oxygen that keeps all animals, including human beings, alive. (There is a bit of carbon dioxide in the air, too. Air is $1/3000$ carbon dioxide.)

Once Lavoisier had worked that out, the next question was why all the breathing and all the fires on Earth didn't use up all the oxygen and replace it with carbon dioxide? If that happened, all breathing creatures would die and nothing would burn. Yet there continued to be plenty of breathing and fires, and plenty of oxygen in the air, too.

It seemed that something replaced the oxygen in the air as quickly as it was used up. But what?

The beginning of an answer had come with Priestley. In 1771, Priestley placed a mouse in a closed container of air. Eventually the mouse used up so much of the oxygen in its breathing that it couldn't live on what was left, and it died.

Priestley wondered if plants would also die in such

Antoine Lavoisier

air. He removed the mouse, and put a sprig of mint in a glass of water into the closed container in which the mouse had died.

The little plant did *not* die. It grew in the container for months and did fine. What was more, at the end of that time, Priestley put a mouse into the container and it lived and ran about. What's more, a candle burned in the container.

Priestley did not quite understand what had happened, since he had not yet discovered oxygen. Once Lavoisier had worked out the nature of air, however, all was clear. While animals used up the oxygen in the air, plants somehow put it back. As long as Earth was covered with plant life, oxygen would never be used up. This was reassuring to scientists of that time, but not so cheering today when thousands of acres of rainforests are being leveled for farming and the demand for wood products is clearing trees away.

Joseph Priestley

2
Light and Carbohydrates

WHEN OXYGEN COMBINES with substances in the human body to produce carbon dioxide and water, it also produces *energy* (EN-er-jee). This term is from Greek words meaning "contains work," because energy makes it possible to do work. The *chemical energy* (KEM-ih-kul) obtained from the combination of oxygen and body substances makes it possible for us to move and do all the things we do.

In Priestley's time, scientists didn't quite understand about energy, but later on much was discovered about it. If combining oxygen with carbon and hydrogen atoms to form carbon dioxide and water produced energy, what about the reverse? What about forming oxygen again and putting it back in the air. Eventually, scientists learned that the energy situation would also reverse. Oxygen formation would *use up* energy. This meant that if plants formed oxygen they had to get energy to make that possible. Where did the energy come from?

A Dutch scientist, Jan Ingenhousz (ING-en-hows, 1730–1799), found the answer. He kept studying the way in which plants formed oxygen and, in 1779, noticed that this only happened in the light. Plants formed no oxygen in the dark.

Sunlight contains energy, and this energy makes it possible for plants to grow and manufacture within themselves the complicated substances that animals use as food. The energy from sunlight also makes it possible for plants to form oxygen.

The process of making complicated substances out of simple ones is called *synthesis* (SIN-thuh-sis) by scientists. It is from Greek words meaning "to put together." When light energy is used to make this possible, the process is "photosynthesis" (FOH-toh-SIN-thuh-sis), meaning "to put together by light."

Photosynthesis is the most important chemical process on Earth. It produces the food and oxygen that all animals, including human beings, live on.

The question still remained, though, as to what the source of carbon atoms was, since water supplied only hydrogen and oxygen atoms.

A Swiss scientist, Jean Senebier (seh-neh-BYAY, 1742–1809), in 1782, was the first to suggest that the source had to be the carbon dioxide in the air.

In 1804, another Swiss scientist, Nicolas Theodore

de Saussure (soh-SYOOR, 1767–1845), repeated Helmont's experiment. This time, though, he carefully supplied the plant with carbon dioxide as well as water. He measured how much of each was used up, and how much weight the plant gained. He was able to show that the plant substance was indeed built up of carbon dioxide and water.

Now then, this is the way it looks. In plants: *carbon dioxide + water + light energy = food + oxygen* (photosynthesis).

In animals: *food + oxygen = carbon dioxide + water + chemical energy* (respiration).

Photosynthesis and respiration work in opposite directions. What happens is that light energy is turned into chemical energy. The light energy is used up, but food and oxygen are not. Nor need we worry about light energy, for the Sun has delivered it for billions of years and will go on to deliver it for additional billions of years.

Of the substances involved in photosynthesis and respiration, carbon dioxide, water, and oxygen are quite simple. Each is composed of small *molecules* (MOL-uh-kyoolz), which are combinations of atoms. A carbon dioxide molecule is made up of one carbon atom and two oxygen atoms. A water molecule is made up of two hydrogen atoms and one oxygen atom. An oxygen molecule is made up of two oxygen atoms.

Food, however, and the material out of which living creatures are made have quite complicated molecules.

In 1815, a British scientist, William Prout (1785–1850), was the first to divide food materials into three main groups. Today we call these groups: carbohydrates (KAHR-boh-HY-drayts), fats, and proteins (PRO-teenz). Carbohydrates and fats both have rather large molecules that include carbon, hydrogen, and oxygen atoms. Proteins have particularly large molecules that contain not only carbon, hydrogen, and oxygen atoms, but nitrogen and sulfur atoms as well, together with an occasional scattering of other types of atoms.

Of these three varieties, the most common in plants is carbohydrates. All plants contain *cellulose* (SELL-yoo-lohs), which is a carbohydrate that is the principal substance in wood. Cellulose is firm and strong and supports the plants. Another common type of carbohydrate is starch, which is soft and easily digested. It is the principal food stored in plants.

Once a plant has a supply of carbohydrates, it can easily make fat out of it, fat being a particularly concentrated form of food. A plant can also make protein out of carbohydrates, with the help of minerals that it absorbs from the water or the soil.

Because plants contain so much in the way of carbohydrate, and because carbohydrate can be used to form fat and protein without light energy, it seems reasonable to suppose that photosynthesis forms carbohydrates. Everything else in the plant is then made out of carbohydrate in ordinary chemical ways that work in animals, too.

This was shown by a German scientist, Julius von Sachs (ZAHKS, 1832–1897). In 1868, his first discovery about plants was that, in the dark, they combine oxygen with the material in their bodies and produce carbon dioxide and water in order to make use of

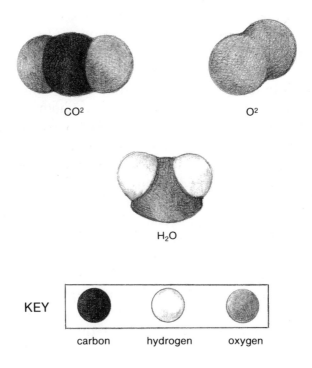

Carbon Dioxide, Oxygen and Water Molecules

chemical energy, just as animals do. <u>In the light, however, photosynthesis produces far more food and oxygen than plants need for their own use and that is</u> why there is always plenty for animals to eat and breathe.

Then, in 1872, Sachs kept a plant in the dark long enough to have it combine most of its substance with oxygen. By then, it was ready to have photosynthesis manufacture more food quickly. Sachs exposed the plant to sunlight, but covered part of the leaves with dark paper through which sunlight couldn't pass.

As it happens, starch combines with iodine fumes to form a black compound. After the leaves had been exposed to sunlight for just a little while, Sachs removed the black paper and exposed the leaves to iodine fumes. The parts of the leaves that had been exposed to the sunlight turned black at once. They were filled with starch that had been quickly formed by photosynthesis. The parts of the leaves that had been covered with paper did not turn black. They contained no starch.

Even though photosynthesis produces carbohydrates so quickly, it may not be starch that is formed first.

That thought arises because starch molecules are huge, and consist of chains of hundreds of smaller molecules. What's more, it is easy to break down starch into the individual units of the chain.

Small fragments of starch molecules are *sugars*, and the most common sugar of all is a single link of the chain-molecule that makes up starch. That single link is called *glucose* (GLOO-kose).

WHAT HAPPENS WHEN PUT IN DARK READ

Von Sachs' Experiment

Cellulose has a molecule that is an even longer chain of small molecules than starch is, but in cellulose the small molecule is *also* glucose. The difference is that the glucose molecules are linked together in different ways. In starch, the links are easily broken and when this happens in the body, we say the starch is *digested*.

Cellulose molecules are linked in a much firmer way and it is hard to break them down into glucose units. Cellulose can only be digested by certain one-celled animals. (Such one-celled animals live in the intestines of termites, and that is why termites can live on wood.)

In animals, including human beings, chemical energy can be obtained from either carbohydrates, fats, or proteins. In every case, though, before energy is obtained, the substances are broken down or changed into glucose. The glucose enters the bloodstream and is carried to all parts of the body. Glucose is *the* substance used for chemical energy.

It seems reasonable to suppose, then, that what is formed by photosynthesis is glucose. The plant can rapidly combine glucose into starch, change the starch into cellulose if it needs to, or concentrate it into fat, or add minerals to make it into protein. Glucose has a medium-sized molecule, made up of six carbon atoms, twelve hydrogen atoms, and six oxygen atoms, so it, too, may not be the very first substance formed by photosynthesis, as we will see later.

DRAW
DIAGRAM

Glucose Molecule

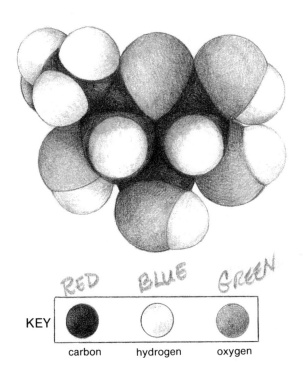

RED   BLUE   GREEN

KEY | ● | ○ | ● |
| carbon | hydrogen | oxygen |

3
Chlorophyll

BUT NOW THERE arises another question. (There are always other questions. No matter how much scientists discover, there are always additional puzzles. That's what makes science fun.)

Why is it that plants can photosynthesize and animals can't? It must be that plants have something animals don't have.

What about the matter of color? Plants are green or, at least, have important green parts. Animals are never truly green. (There are birds with green feathers, but feather-green is made up of completely different chemicals than plant-green.)

Is it really important that plants are green? It must

be. There are some living things that are like plants in many ways. They seem to have the same structures, many of the same chemical substances, and so on. Yet these plants are not green. Examples are mushrooms. Such nongreen plants do not photosynthesize.

Even plants that are green only photosynthesize in those parts that have the green color. A tree, for instance, does not photosynthesize in its roots, bark, branches, or twigs, but only in its green leaves.

In 1817, two French scientists, Pierre Joseph Pelletier (pel-TYAY, 1788–1842) and Joseph Bienaime Caventou (ka-vahn-TOO, 1795–1877), isolated the green substance from plants. They named it *chlorophyll* (KLAW-roh-fil) from Greek words meaning "green leaf."

The chlorophyll molecule, however, was a very complicated one, and, for nearly a century, scientists could find out little about it. Naturally, they did their best because they were quite certain that it was this substance, which existed in green plants but not in animals, that made photosynthesis possible.

Finally, in 1906, answers began to come. This was through the investigations of a German scientist, Richard Willstätter (VIL-shtet-ter, 1872–1942). He was the first to prepare chlorophyll in pure form and to study it in detail.

He found that it was not a single substance, but two substances with very similar molecules. He called one of them "chlorophyll *a*." It made up three-fourths of the chlorophyll in plants. The other, which made up the remaining quarter, he called "chlorophyll *b*."

Willstätter then studied the kinds of atoms that made up the chlorophyll molecules. He found that carbon, hydrogen, oxygen, and nitrogen atoms were present. This was not surprising. Almost every molecule in living things contain carbon, hydrogen, and oxygen atoms, and most of them contain nitrogen atoms as well.

However, he also found atoms of an element called "magnesium" (mag-NEE-zee-um). This was a surprise. Chlorophyll was the first molecule from living beings that was found to contain magnesium atoms.

Willstätter then showed that chlorophyll *a* had a molecule built up of fifty-five carbon atoms, seventy-two hydrogen atoms, four nitrogen atoms, five oxygen atoms, and one magnesium atom. Chlorophyll *b* was almost the same but had only seventy hydrogen atoms and it had six oxygen atoms.

Willstätter was not able to work out the exact arrangement of all those atoms. He did find out, though, that the molecule contained small rings of atoms, with four carbon atoms and one nitrogen atom in each ring. Such an arrangement is called a *pyrrole ring* (PIR-ole). For his work, Willstätter received a Nobel Prize in chemistry in 1915.

Another German scientist, Hans Fischer (1881–1945), carried on the work. He showed that four pyrrole rings could be put together in one large ring called a *porphyrin ring* (PAWR-fih-rin). By having an atom of iron in the center of the porphyrin ring and by having some chains of atoms attached to the rim of the ring, he worked out the structure of a compound called *heme* (HEEM), which gives the red color to blood. He did this in 1930 and received the Nobel Prize for chemistry that same year.

It turned out that chlorophyll rather resembled heme. Chlorophyll had a magnesium atom at the center of the porphyrin ring, instead of iron, and in chlorophyll the chains of atoms attached to the rim were different and more complicated than in heme, but Fischer managed to work it all out.

The final proof came in 1960, when an American scientist, Robert Burns Woodward (1917–1979), actually put together all the proper atoms in the proper way, in just the order that Fischer had said they ought to be arranged. Woodward ended with something that acted exactly like chlorophyll obtained from green plants.

That meant that Fischer's structure was absolutely right, and for this (and other important work) Woodward received the Nobel Prize in chemistry in 1965.

You might think that once scientists had obtained chlorophyll from green plants, they could use the substance to bring about photosynthesis. Suppose you dissolved chlorophyll in water and bubbled carbon dioxide through it. Should not the carbon dioxide combine with the water in the presence of chlorophyll to form glucose and then starch?

Well, perhaps it should, but it doesn't. Chlorophyll works well inside the plant, but it doesn't work outside the plant.

Why should that be? Because, in the plant, chlorophyll is part of a complicated system, and it is only

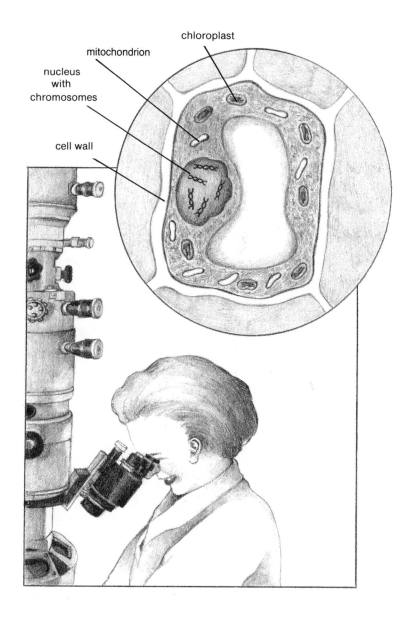

chloroplast

mitochondrion

nucleus
with
chromosomes

cell wall

Plant cell as seen under an electron microscope

the chlorophyll system that works, not the chlorophyll by itself.

All plants and animals are made up of cells about 1/750 of an inch across. Some tiny plants and animals are made up of only a single cell each and are so small they can only be seen in a microscope. Large plants and animals are made up of cells that are just as tiny, but there are a great many of those cells. A human being is made up of some fifty trillion (50,000,000,000,000) cells.

The cell, small as it is, is not just a blob of material. It is made up of still smaller objects called *organelles* (awr-guh-NELLZ). For instance, each cell has a small body called the *nucleus* (NYOO-klee-us) that contains many stubby little *chromosomes* (KROH-moh-somez). The chromosomes control the way in which a cell divides into two cells. It also controls the way in which physical characteristics are passed from the original cell to the two cells that form from it, and from parents to children.

In 1898, a German scientist, Carl Benda, found that, outside the nucleus, the cell has many small bodies which he named *mitochondria* (My-toh-KON-dree-uh). A single one is called a *mitochondrion*.

With time, it was discovered that the mitochondria are responsible for respiration. Every cell with the ability to combine oxygen and glucose to form chemical energy has mitochondria, and it is in the mitochondria that the combining takes place.

The average mitochondrion is shaped like a very tiny football, about 1/1000 of an inch long and

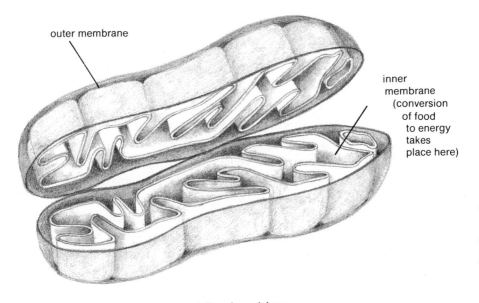

outer membrane

inner membrane (conversion of food to energy takes place here)

Mitochondrion

1/25,000 of an inch wide. There might be anywhere from several hundred to several thousand in each cell.

In the 1930s, scientists invented the *electron microscope,* which can be used to study objects too small to see in ordinary microscopes. It was then found that even the mitochondrion has a very complex structure. In it are arranged a number of special protein molecules, called *enzymes* (EN-zimez). Each enzyme can bring about a particular chemical change. All of them, working together, bring about a whole series of changes that finally result in combining glucose and oxygen to form chemical energy.

But if there is an organelle, the mitochondrion, that exists in both plant and animal cells to bring about respiration, is there another organelle, in plant cells only, that brings about photosynthesis?

The answer is yes. In 1883, Julius von Sachs, who had shown that photosynthesis formed starch, found that the chlorophyll in plant cells is not spread through the entire cell. It is found in one or more organelles within the cell. Such organelles were eventually called *chloroplasts* (KLAW-roh-plasts).

The chloroplast is two or three times as long and thick as a mitochondrion. Its structure is even more complicated than that of the mitochondrion. Under the electron microscope, you can see that the chloroplast is made up of tiny units, each one of which may contain 250 to 300 chlorophyll molecules. There are also present many enzymes that bring about certain reactions.

That is why a single chlorophyll molecule can't photosynthesize all by itself. It has to work in groups, and the enzymes have to be present too.

If a cell is broken up, intact mitochondria can be obtained pretty easily. The chloroplasts, being larger and more complicated, are also more fragile. Usually, when the plant cell is broken up, the chloroplasts also break into pieces, and the individual pieces do not photosynthesize by themselves.

Not until 1954, was a Polish-American scientist, Daniel I. Arnon (born, 1910), able to break up plant cells so gently that whole chloroplasts could be obtained that could carry through photosynthesis.

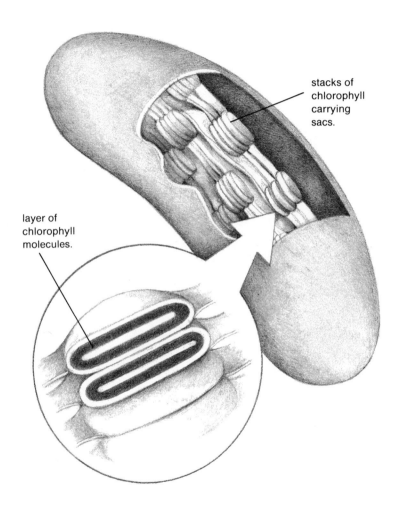

stacks of
chlorophyll
carrying
sacs.

layer of
chlorophyll
molecules.

Chloroplast

4
Intermediates

BUT WHY MUST mitochondria and chloroplasts be so complicated? Why can't mitochondria just combine glucose and oxygen and get carbon dioxide and water—bang? Why can't chloroplasts just combine carbon dioxide and water and get glucose and oxygen—bang? It would be so simple.

For one thing, if glucose were combined with oxygen all in one step, too much energy would be produced at one time. The cells couldn't handle it all. If carbon dioxide and water were combined all in one step, too much energy would be required at one time. The cells couldn't supply it all.

Instead, in both cases, the reaction goes little by little. One small change is followed by another small change, so that energy is produced in small amounts, or used up in small amounts. The cells can handle the small amounts in either direction.

This means that all the little changes must be controlled. None must go too quickly, none too slowly, and they must go in the right order. This means that each change must be controlled by an enzyme of its own. Mitochondria and chloroplasts have to be carefully organized, so that everything will work smoothly.

The little changes produce a whole series of molecules in between glucose at one end and carbon dioxide and water at the other end, in either direction. These molecules are called *intermediates* (in-ter-MEE-dee-its). These exist only in tiny quantities because they are sent on to the next stop and used up almost as quickly as they are formed.

In 1905, a British scientist, Arthur Harden (1865–1940), was studying the way in which certain cells broke down glucose to alcohol and carbon dioxide. This change does not involve oxygen and is simpler than respiration, but it is closely related to it, and it is done in steps.

The fact that glucose was breaking down could be seen by the appearance of bubbles of carbon dioxide in the water where the cells were floating. After a while, though, the bubbling slowed and stopped. The cells were still alive and there was still plenty of glucose present, so why should everything have stopped?

Harden felt that something required for breaking down the glucose had been used up. He tried adding different substances to the mixture. To his surprise, he found that when a small quantity of a mineral called a *phosphate* (FOS-fate) was added, the bubbling started again. Phosphates contain atoms of the element *phosphorus* (FOS-fuh-rus). Until then no one had thought that phosphorus had anything to do with glucose breakdown.

Harden examined the glucose mixture for any substance that might contain phosphorus atoms. He found that glucose had been altered into a very similar sugar called *fructose* (FROOK-tose) and that to the molecules of fructose were added two phosphate groups. This compound was called *fructose diphosphate* (FROOK-tose-dy-FOS-fate), and it was the first intermediate found in glucose breakdown or formation.

For this discovery, Harden received a Nobel Prize in chemistry in 1929.

After that, a number of other intermediates were discovered. Little by little, a long chain of steps going from glucose and oxygen to carbon dioxide and water was worked out. It was found that many of these intermediates have phosphate groups attached and these phosphates are very useful when it comes to transferring energy from molecule to molecule in convenient and usable amounts.

If we broke down the glucose without the phosphate intermediates, it would be like getting a hundred dollar bill. This would be a sizable sum of money, but it might be useless to us. If we tried to buy a bar of candy, or get on a bus, the store dealer, or the bus

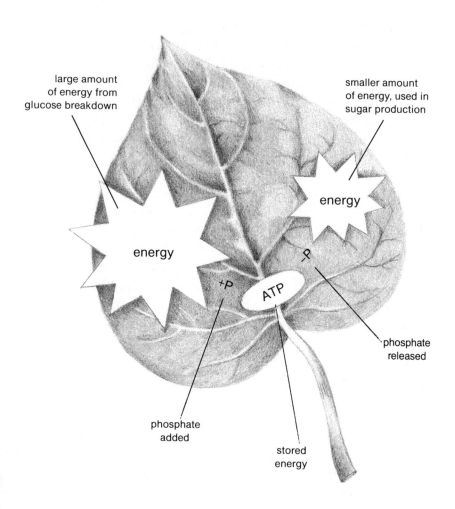

large amount
of energy from
glucose breakdown

smaller amount
of energy, used in
sugar production

energy

energy

+P

ATP

-P

phosphate
released

phosphate
added

stored
energy

driver, might not have change and wouldn't take it.

If, however, we went to a bank and changed the hundred dollar bill into tens, fives, and ones, then the same hundred dollars would be much more useful. Everyone would take the small bills.

The phosphate intermediates offer the cells small bits of energy, and the body can use them easily. One intermediate, *adenosine triphosphate* (ad-eh-NO-seen-try-FOS-fate), which is usually abbreviated *ATP*, is particularly useful. At almost every point in the body where energy is needed, ATP is used.

It was much easier to work out the steps of respiration than of photosynthesis, however.

For one thing, respiration is easily made to take place in pieces, so that it can be studied in detail, a little bit here, a little bit there. All of it can then be put together like a jigsaw puzzle. Photosynthesis, however, will only work with intact chloroplasts and the result is then so complicated that it is almost impossible to work out the details.

Then, too, scientists managed to get started on the wrong path.

After all, if we breathe in oxygen and breathe out carbon dioxide, the oxygen must combine with carbon in the substances of the body to form the carbon dioxide. That is certainly correct. Oxygen also combines with hydrogen in the substances of the body to form water, but scientists didn't seem to attach much importance to water. Water makes up at least two-thirds of the weight of living things. A little bit more or less water in the breath doesn't seem to matter.

So scientists concentrated on carbon dioxide. If, in

respiration, oxygen and carbon combined to form carbon dioxide, they felt sure that in photosynthesis the opposite must take place. Carbon dioxide must be pulled apart by photosynthesis, producing a carbon atom and also two oxygen atoms, which would combine to form an oxygen molecule. The oxygen molecules would be released into the air, and six carbon atoms would combine with water to form glucose.

Scientists thought this was so until 1937.

In that year, a British scientist, Robert Hill, isolated chloroplasts from leaves. The chloroplasts were damaged in the process and wouldn't photosynthesize. Hill thought something had been lost by the chloroplasts, so he tried to add different things that might make up for the loss. Certain molecules containing iron are important in respiration and Hill thought they might be important in photosynthesis, too. He therefore added small iron-containing molecules to his damaged chloroplasts.

When he did so, the chloroplasts started forming oxygen as they would if they were photosynthesizing. If the oxygen came from broken carbon dioxide molecules, as scientists thought they would, the carbon ought to have combined with water to form glucose, and then starch. However, no glucose or starch formed—only oxygen.

This might mean that the oxygen might have come, not from breaking carbon dioxide molecules apart, but by breaking water molecules apart. If it were water molecules that were broken, and if nothing else happened, there would be no carbon atoms to form glucose and starch.

How could anyone be completely sure, though, from which molecules oxygen comes. Oxygen is oxygen, and you can't tell by looking at it what kind of molecule it comes from.

But it turned out that you can, in certain ways. By 1912, it was realized that not all the atoms of an element are alike. They all behave the same way, chemically, but some are a little heavier than others. In 1929, for instance, an American scientist, William Francis Giauque (jee-OKE, 1895–1982), found that most oxygen atoms are of the same type, one called *oxygen-16*. But there are small quantities of the heavier *oxygen-18* also present.

As time went on, scientists learned how to separate the two types of oxygen. They could make water with molecules containing a good deal of oxygen-18.

In 1941, a Canadian-American scientist, Martin David Kamen (born, 1913), watered photosynthesizing plants with water containing a good deal of oxygen-18. The plants were also exposed to ordinary carbon dioxide that contained oxygen-16, but almost no oxygen-18.

Kamen next studied the oxygen produced by the plants. If the oxygen was almost all oxygen-16, it had to come from the carbon dioxide. If the oxygen contained a considerable quantity of oxygen-18, it had to come from the water.

It turned out that the oxygen produced contained oxygen-18 in just the amount that would be expected if it came from the water molecule.

That settled the matter. What happens in photosynthesis is that light energy is used by the plant to break

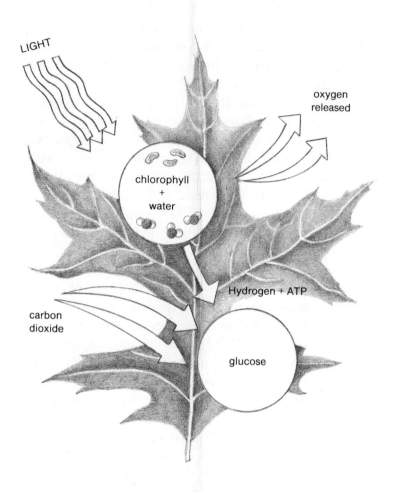

LIGHT

oxygen released

chlorophyll
+
water

Hydrogen + ATP

carbon dioxide

glucose

Photosynthesis

the water molecule into hydrogen atoms and oxygen atoms. Then, if the chloroplasts are intact and contain all their enzymes, the hydrogen combines with carbon dioxide to form glucose and starch, while the oxygen passes into the air.

Scientists still needed to know the details of what happens after the water molecule is split. They were quite sure that molecules containing phosphates had to be involved, but how were they to find out exactly what molecules these were?

The trouble with working with oxygen-18 is that it takes a long time to separate and identify it, while the photosynthesis intermediates form and disappear very quickly. What's more, you need quite a bit of the intermediate to isolate enough oxygen-18 to work with, and the intermediates exist in only tiny quantities. What scientists had to have was something they could detect in very small quantities and very quickly.

In 1934, two French scientists, Frédéric Joliot-Curie (zho-lyoh-kyoo-REE, 1900–1958) and his wife, Irène (1897–1956), found that it is possible to make some atom varieties that are *radioactive*. These break down to other atoms, giving up certain radiations. The radiations are easy to detect so that radioactive varieties of atoms can be very easily and quickly detected and identified even if present in only tiny amounts. For this work, the Joliot-Curies got a Nobel Prize in chemistry in 1935.

There are radioactive varieties of oxygen and of hydrogen, but they break down and disappear in only minutes, so that any experiment that uses them has to be carried through and completed in a very short time. There is a radioactive carbon variety, called *carbon-11*, that also breaks down rapidly and is therefore difficult to use.

But in 1939, Kamen, who had first proved that light energy in photosynthesis splits the water molecule, made another discovery. He found a kind of carbon, called *carbon-14*, that is radioactive but that breaks down so slowly it can last thousands of years.

Carbon atoms are the most important atoms in living things, and now it was possible to trace the intermediates in photosynthesis by using carbon-14.

To do this, scientists would have to expose plants to light and to carbon dioxide containing a great many carbon-14 atoms. The plants could then be mashed up and scientists would have to identify just which molecules contained carbon-14. Those molecules would have been formed through photosynthesis.

Still, it's not easy to separate small quantities of many different molecules. In 1944, however, a method was worked out by two British scientists, Archer John Porter Martin (born, 1910) and Richard Laurence Millington Synge (born, 1914). They showed that if a mixture of molecules is allowed to soak upward through a piece of porous paper, each different molecule will move upward at a different speed. In time they will all be separated.

This was called *paper chromatography* (KROH-muh-TOG-ruh-fee). Martin and Synge received a Nobel Prize in chemistry in 1953 for this discovery.

Now experiments could be run in which photosynthesizing plants were exposed to carbon dioxide with carbon-14, and the mixture of chemicals that were

Paper Chromatography

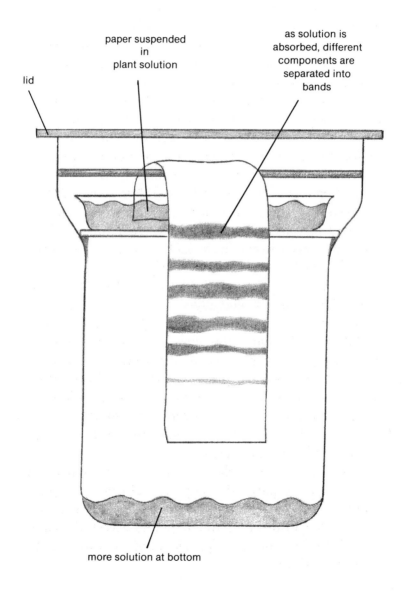

lid

paper suspended
in
plant solution

as solution is
absorbed, different
components are
separated into
bands

more solution at bottom

produced could be separated by paper chromatography. Scientists could easily tell which of the separated chemicals contained carbon-14. Then, because carbon-14 lasted such a long time, scientists could work slowly and carefully to identify each molecule without losing its carbon-14 marker.

At first, the experiments worked too well. A very complicated mixture was formed and separated by paper chromatography. However, so many different molecules containing carbon-14 were found that scientists could not tell which were formed first.

An American scientist, Melvin Calvin (born, 1911), realized that the trick was to let the photosynthesis proceed for just a few seconds. In that time, only a few substances would have had a chance to be produced, and they would be the early ones.

Calvin began his studies in 1948 and made use of one-celled plants called *algae* (AL-jee) that grew in water. The algae were exposed to light and to ordinary carbon dioxide. Once the algae were photosynthesizing actively, they were drained through a long glass tube into hot alcohol, which killed them. While they were passing through the tube, carbon dioxide containing carbon-14 was bubbled through the water. The algae had only five seconds to work with the carbon-14 before they were killed.

The algae were mashed up and the substances in them were separated by paper chromatography. About ninety percent of all the carbon-14 was found in a single substance. That compound was studied and found to be *phosphoglyceric acid* (FOS-foh-glih-SEHR-ik-AS-id).

Melvin Calvin

Phosphoglyceric acid has a molecule containing three carbon atoms. Calvin could even work out which carbon atom was carbon-14. That made it possible to see just how the phosphoglyceric acid was formed.

Continuing experiments finally explained many of the detailed changes in photosynthesis in what turned out to be a very complicated pattern. For his work, Calvin received a Nobel Prize in chemistry in 1961.

We know much, much more about photosynthesis than we did two centuries ago when Priestley first found that plants produced oxygen. However, we still don't know all the details.

And we still can't figure out some simpler way to duplicate what green plants do in their complicated chloroplasts. If we could, we might be able to produce vast quantities of sugar, starch, and other foodstuffs, just making use of the energy of sunlight on carbon dioxide and water. That would help feed the people of the world.

We have a great deal to learn before we can do that, though.

5
The
Beginning

HOW DID PHOTOSYNTHESIS get started in the first place? Scientists don't exactly know, because they weren't there when it happened. However, they can reason how photosynthesis might have gotten started.

When Earth was first formed, about four and a half billion years ago, there was no life on it. So in the air there couldn't have been any oxygen.

Oxygen is a very active substance. It combines easily with many other kinds of atoms. If, suddenly, there was no life on Earth, the oxygen that is now in the air would combine with different atoms in the soil and, little by little, it would vanish. The only reason oxygen exists now is that photosynthesis keeps making it out of water molecules. In the days when no life existed on Earth, there was no photosynthesis, so there was also no oxygen.

The two planets closest to Earth are Mars and Venus. Each has air, but no life. As a result each has air that consists of nitrogen and carbon dioxide, but no oxygen. Perhaps, in Earth's very early days, its air also consisted of nitrogen and carbon dioxide.

Venus is too hot to have liquid water and Mars is too cold to have it. Earth's temperature, however, is just right, so it has large oceans of water, and that makes all the difference. Because of the oceans, Earth's air has quantities of water vapor. In addition, there might have been some other gases present in the beginning, gases such as *methane* (meh-THAYN) and *ammonia* (uh-MOH-nyuh). Methane has molecules made up of one carbon atom and four hydrogen atoms. Ammonia has molecules made up of one nitrogen atom and three hydrogen atoms.

Nitrogen, carbon dioxide, water, methane, and ammonia all have small molecules. These molecules can combine in different ways to form larger molecules, provided energy is added. There must have been, on the early Earth, energy sources such as lightning and volcanic heat. Most important of all, probably, was sunlight, particularly an energetic kind called *ultraviolet light* (UL-truh-VI-oh-let), which we can't see but which has enough energy to give us sunburn.

In 1952, an American scientist, Stanley Lloyd Miller (born, 1930), took a mixture of simple gases such as may have been in Earth's early air and passed electric sparks through it as an energy source. After a

Earth before life developed

week, he found that small molecules had combined into larger ones.

Later, other people experimented in the same fashion and some interesting larger molecules were formed. These included *amino acids* (uh-MEE-noh-AS-idz), which can combine into protein molecules. There were also *nucleotides* (NYOO-klee-oh-TIDEZ), which can combine into nucleic acid molecules. It is possible that porphyrin rings of atoms can also be formed in the same way.

These compounds are all very important, because proteins include enzymes that control all the chemical changes in living things. Nucleic acids control cell division and transmit physical characteristics. Porphyrin rings are key portions of chemicals that make respiration and photosynthesis possible.

An American scientist, Sidney Walter Fox (born, 1912), showed that if amino acids are warmed, they combine into protein-like molecules. These clump together into little spheres that look and act very much like cells.

It may be, then, that on the early Earth, such protein cells formed. They were built up from small molecules by ultraviolet light, and some were more lifelike than others. Perhaps the more lifelike fed on the less lifelike.

Such protein cells were simple and clumsy things and couldn't divide and multiply very well. There may also have been clumps of nucleic acid that could divide very well indeed but could hardly do anything else for lack of enzymes.

There came a time, perhaps, when protein cells

and nucleic acid cells combined. Then new cells were formed that were much more efficient. They could divide well and they could perform many other functions. They may have formed as early as three and a half billion years ago, and they are called *prokaryotes* (PROH-ka-ree-otes). They were the ancestors of the bacteria that still live today, but the early prokaryotes were probably considerably simpler than most modern bacteria.

However, the air was changing. Ultraviolet light from the Sun split water-vapor molecules in the upper air into hydrogen and oxygen. The hydrogen atoms were so small and light that Earth's gravity couldn't hold them and they escaped into space. The oxygen atoms remained in the upper air and the ultraviolet light forced them into a high energy combination of three atoms to a molecule instead of the *two* in ordinary oxygen. This three-atom molecule is called *ozone* (OH-zone).

Ordinary oxygen lets ultraviolet light pass through, but ozone does not. This meant that, as the ozone layer built up in the upper air, less and less ultraviolet light reached the surface of Earth. Simple molecules were built up in smaller quantities, and the living cells began to suffer a shortage of food and to starve.

However, porphyrin ring compounds had formed and clumped together. They could absorb the energy of ordinary visible light that could pass through ozone without trouble. At first the porphyrins used the light in a very clumsy fashion, but those that used it more efficiently built up food in their own neighborhood and lived better. Millions of years passed and the use

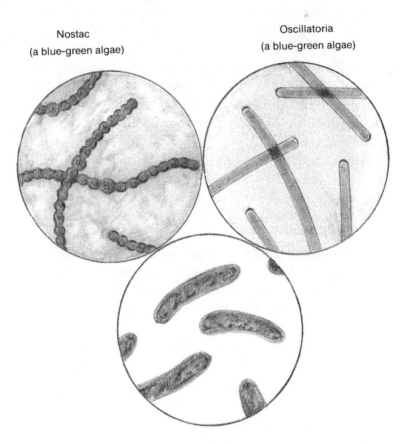

Nostac
(a blue-green algae)

Oscillatoria
(a blue-green algae)

Rhodospirillum rubrum

Prokaryotes

(microscopic views)

of visible light became more and more efficient, until the porphyrin cell developed molecules that were growing more and more like chlorophyll. They were becoming something like chloroplasts. There are still tiny bacteria-like cells today that seem to be nothing more than a chloroplast. They are *cyanobacteria* (SY-uh-noh-bak-TEE-ree-uh) and are a second form of prokaryote.

The chloroplasts broke up water molecules to use the hydrogen atoms to form food. The oxygen atoms got into the air and slowly began to accumulate there. Most forms of primitive life couldn't handle the active molecules of oxygen and were slowly poisoned.

However, some porphyrin clumps developed enzymes that could make use of oxygen and extract energy by combining it with carbon and hydrogen. They were the ancestors of modern mitochondria, and still another form of prokaryote.

For over two billion years prokaryotes were the only form of life that existed on Earth.

Little by little, though, prokaryotes combined to form larger, more complicated cells. Cells that contained nucleic acids and proteins combined with chloroplasts and mitochondria to resemble modern plant cells. Some combined only with mitochondria to become animal cells. Both kinds are called *eukaryotes* (YOO-ka-ree-otes).

In the last billion years, these eukaryotes have been the most important forms of life. Beginning about 800 million years ago, they combined into animals and plants made up of many cells. These were "multicellular" (MUL-tee-SELL-yoo-ler) creatures.

Interdependence of Plants and Animals

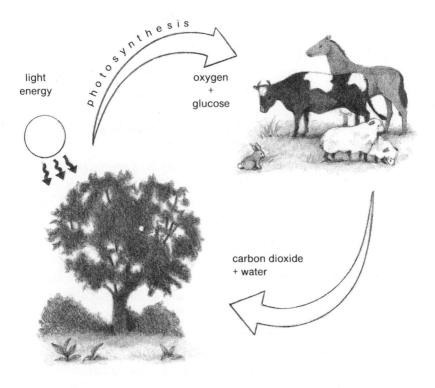

light
energy

p h o t o s y n t h e s i s

oxygen
+
glucose

carbon dioxide
+ water

The world is now full of multicellular plants and animals—whales, oak trees, human beings, butterflies, roses, and so on. However, one-celled plants and animals still exist, and prokaryotes too. In fact, there are even bacteria that can't live in the presence of oxygen, and that never seem to have added mitochondria to their cells.

Except for those few bacteria that can't live on oxygen, and other creatures that live on them, all forms of life depend on photosynthesis. Without photosynthesis, Earth would drift back to the way things were billions of years ago, when only the simplest life-forms existed.

This is why ecologists today want to preserve the green growing plains and forests that supply the balance of oxygen to our atmosphere and why environmentalists want to stop the pollution that blocks life-giving sunlight from Earth's surface. Scientists need to keep on asking questions and finding answers to these problems. They will add new chapters to the story of photosynthesis on Earth.

INDEX